# The Ultimate Ukulele
# SCALE CHART

## Introduction

**The Ultimate Ukulele Scale Chart** has been created to assist you in learning to play today's most commonly used scales. It is a fast and fun way to gain instant access to 120 scale patterns—just look up a scale and you can easily find out how and where to play it on the ukulele.

This book will not only show you the different scales and their locations, but it will also provide the fundamentals behind *how* and *why* each scale is constructed (see page 8). This will greatly enhance your playing and understanding of scales.

## How to Use This Book

To use the chart on the following pages, simply find the root of the desired scale (C, D, E, etc.) in the left column, and the scale type (major, minor, etc.) along the top of the chart. Read down and across to locate the correct scale. The fingering patterns are indicated with fretboard diagrams, similar to the sample at right.

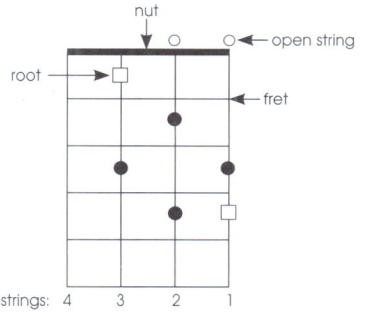

## Playing the Scale Patterns

Begin on the third string, playing each fretted or open note in sequence before moving to the next string. For scales that span four frets, simply use one finger per fret. For scales that extend beyond four frets, you can experiment to see which fingering feels best. Starting fret numbers are provided as the patterns move up the neck.

Each scale pattern shown in this book begins and ends on the root note. (If your ukulele has 12 frets, upper notes of the B♭ and B scales will be inaccessible.) Refer to the standard ukulele fretboard below to find other locations of a particular scale.

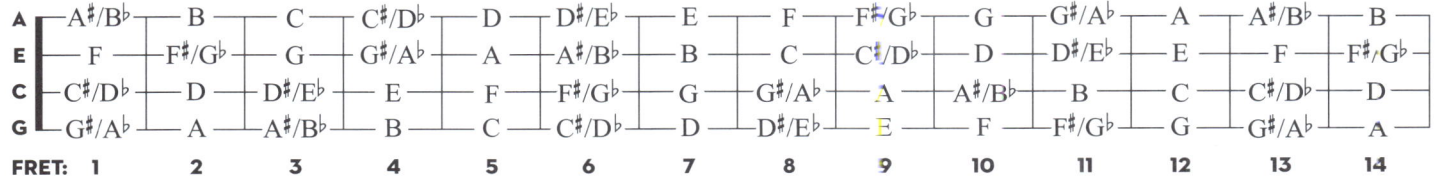

| | FRET: 1 | 2 | 3 | 4 | 5 | 6 | 7 | 8 | 9 | 10 | 11 | 12 | 13 | 14 |
|---|---|---|---|---|---|---|---|---|---|---|---|---|---|---|
| A | A♯/B♭ | B | C | C♯/D♭ | D | D♯/E♭ | E | F | F♯/G♭ | G | G♯/A♭ | A | A♯/B♭ | B |
| E | F | F♯/G♭ | G | G♯/A♭ | A | A♯/B♭ | B | C | C♯/D♭ | D | D♯/E♭ | E | F | F♯/G♭ |
| C | C♯/D♭ | D | D♯/E♭ | E | F | F♯/G♭ | G | G♯/A♭ | A | A♯/B♭ | B | C | C♯/D♭ | D |
| G | G♯/A♭ | A | A♯/B♭ | B | C | C♯/D♭ | D | D♯/E♭ | E | F | F♯/G♭ | G | G♯/A♭ | A |

ISBN 978-1-4803-8543-6

## HAL•LEONARD®
## CORPORATION

7777 W. BLUEMOUND RD. P.O. BOX 13819 MILWAUKEE, WI 53213

In Australia Contact:
**Hal Leonard Australia Pty. Ltd.**
4 Lentara Court
Cheltenham, Victoria, 3192 Australia
Email: ausadmin@halleonard.com.au

Visit Hal Leonard Online at
**www.halleonard.com**

| | MAJOR | MINOR | MAJOR PENTATONIC | MINOR PENTATONIC | HARMONIC MINOR |
|---|---|---|---|---|---|
| **C** | | | | | |
| **C♯/D♭** | | | | | |
| **D** | 2 fr | | 2 fr | 2 fr | |
| **D♯/E♭** | 3 fr | 2 fr | 3 fr | 3 fr | 2 fr |

| | MELODIC MINOR | BLUES | MIXOLYDIAN | DORIAN | LYDIAN |
|---|---|---|---|---|---|
| C | | | | | |
| C♯/D♭ | | | | | |
| D | | | | | |
| D♯/E♭ | | | | | |

| | MAJOR | MINOR | MAJOR PENTATONIC | MINOR PENTATONIC | HARMONIC MINOR |
|---|---|---|---|---|---|
| E | | | | | |
| F | | | | | |
| F#/Gb | | | | | |
| G | | | | | |

| | MELODIC MINOR | BLUES | MIXOLYDIAN | DORIAN | LYDIAN |
|---|---|---|---|---|---|
| **G♯/A♭** | 7 fr | 8 fr | 8 fr | 7 fr | 8 fr |
| **A** | 8 fr | 9 fr | 9 fr | 8 fr | 9 fr |
| **A♯/B♭** | 9 fr | 10 fr | 10 fr | 9 fr | 10 fr |
| **B** | 10 fr | 11 fr | 11 fr | 10 fr | 11 fr |

# ABOUT SCALES

## What Is a Scale?

A **scale** is a series of notes arranged in ascending or descending order. (The word "scale" comes from the Latin *scala*, which means "ladder.") Scales are important to know on the ukulele, especially when creating riffs, licks, and solos.

## How Are Scales Formed?

Scales are constructed using a combination of **whole steps** and **half steps**. (On the ukulele, a half step is the distance of one fret; a whole step is two frets.) Perhaps the most common scale is the **major scale**, shown here in C:

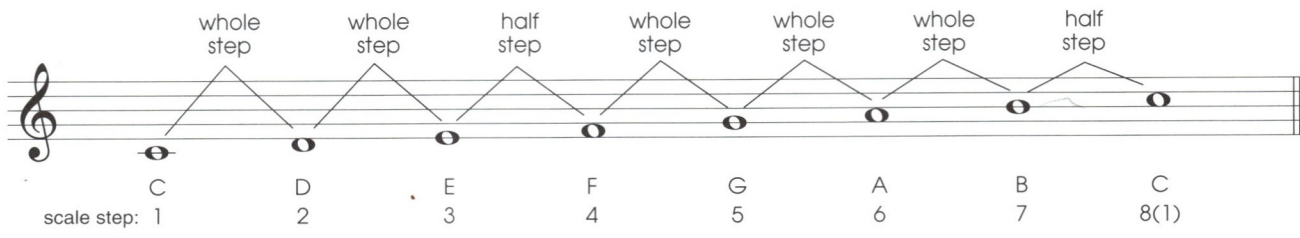

C major scale

| scale step: | C 1 | D 2 | E 3 | F 4 | G 5 | A 6 | B 7 | C 8(1) |

Notice the pattern above: *whole–whole–half–whole–whole–whole–half*. This is the "major scale" step pattern, which can be applied to any root note to create any major scale—C major, D major, E major, etc.

Notice also that each scale step above is numbered: 1-2-3-4-5-6-7. The chart to the right is a construction summary of the scale types in this book (based on the key of C only). Use the numeric formulas to determine the notes of a particular scale. For example, based on a C root, 1–2–♭3–4–5–♭6–♭7 would mean to play C–D–E♭–F–G–A♭–B♭, which is a C minor scale.

| SCALE TYPE | FORMULA | NOTE NAMES |
|---|---|---|
| major | 1-2-3-4-5-6-7 | C-D-E-F-G-A-B |
| minor | 1-2-♭3-4-5-♭6-♭7 | C-D-E♭-F-G-A♭-B♭ |
| major pentatonic | 1-2-3-5-6 | C-D-E-G-A |
| minor pentatonic | 1-♭3-4-5-♭7 | C-E♭-F-G-B♭ |
| harmonic minor | 1-2-♭3-4-5-♭6-7 | C-D-E♭-F-G-A♭-B |
| melodic minor | 1-2-♭3-4-5-6-7* | C-D-E♭-F-G-A-B |
| blues | 1-♭3-4-♭5-5-♭7 | C-E♭-F-G♭-G-B♭ |
| Mixolydian | 1-2-3-4-5-6-♭7 | C-D-E-F-G-A-B♭ |
| Dorian | 1-2-♭3-4-5-6-♭7 | C-D-E♭-F-G-A-B♭ |
| Lydian | 1-2-3-♯4-5-6-7 | C-D-E-F♯-G-A-B |

*Ascending formula only. Descending formula uses ♭7 and ♭6.

## How Are Scales Used?

Here are a few points to keep in mind when improvising with scales:

- You don't need to play scales from root to root; this is simply the way that they are best demonstrated. The notes of a scale can be played *in any order*, and you don't need to use them all. The root is often the most important note.

- Try to choose a scale that goes with the overall key of a song, or song section, not just with a single chord; this will allow you to improvise most effectively, using a single scale pattern.

- In general, when playing in a *major key*, try any of the following scales:
  **major, major pentatonic, blues, Mixolydian, or Lydian.**

  When playing in a *minor key*, try these:
  **minor, minor pentatonic, harmonic minor, melodic minor, blues, or Dorian.**

| | MELODIC MINOR | BLUES | MIXOLYDIAN | DORIAN | LYDIAN |
|---|---|---|---|---|---|
| **E** | | | | | |
| **F** | | | | | |
| **F♯/G♭** | | | | | |
| **G** | | | | | |

| | MAJOR | MINOR | MAJOR PENTATONIC | MINOR PENTATONIC | HARMONIC MINOR |
|---|---|---|---|---|---|
| G#/Ab | 8 fr | 7 fr | 8 fr | 8 fr | 7 fr |
| A | 9 fr | 8 fr | 9 fr | 9 fr | 8 fr |
| A#/Bb | 10 fr | 9 fr | 10 fr | 10 fr | 9 fr |
| B | 11 fr | 10 fr | 11 fr | 11 fr | 10 fr |